Predictive Cyber Threat Analysis using Data Science

An Overview of Possibilities

SA Hale and Terry E. Hale

ISBN: 1546727841
ISBN-13: 978-1546727842

DEDICATION

To all Data Scientists: Keep Digging!

CONTENTS

ACKNOWLEDGMENTS

To all who said No, We thank you.

I. INTRODUCTION

Abstract

Data Science methods can be applied to any imaginable goal and offer insight into how to progress from the status quo to a much higher level of cyber security. This short book addresses some of the possible approaches to applying data science to security needs, how to identify open source tools, and how to potentially implement visualization and statistical analysis for use in the area of Predictive Cyber Threat Analysis.

Because of the vast amount of data that is produced by modern networks, novel methods and techniques are needed to predict cyber threats. The landscape of current threats requires new analysis methods. This paper explores how data science and visualization tools and technology aid in this mission;

allowing the naked eye to detect patterns and obtain insight into our networks. This paper investigates the options available to security engineers, analysts, and investigators for exploiting "big data." We question:

- How is Data Science used to predict cyber threats? What are open source tools available for statistical analysis?
- What methods provide the best visual representation of our analysis?

By developing an understanding of big data, we can adapt to meet the rapid and ever-evolving cyber threat to our national security. Once understood, training, tools, and processes can be implemented in cyber threat analysis.

Our purpose is to help organizations; to develop, a basic understanding of data science, to identify possible tools to used to in data science and security, and finally to focus on applications that can be used to target cyber threats.

"The state of information security is in disarray." (Braxton, 2015). Groups from every industry are failing to detect attacks. A primary cause of today's failures in both security prevention and detection is the ever-increasing amount of data that  networks must process. Data immersion is not a new concept. Experts agree that the phenomenon is accelerating. "Lakes, puddles, and rivers of data have turned to floods and veritable tsunamis of structured, semi-structured, and unstructured data that's streaming from almost every activity that takes place in both the digital and physical worlds" (Pierson, 2015). This is big data, and it is only getting bigger.

Keywords: Data Science, Security, cognitive science, Open Source, visualization, threat analysis, threat intelligence.

II. WHAT IS BIG DATA?

Experts agree that big data is datasets that are too large or not refined (semi-structured or unstructured) or changing too fast to be analyzed using traditional, rational database methodologies.

"What actually distinguishes big data, aside from its volume and variety, is the potential to analyze it to uncover new insights to optimize decision making." (Curry, 2013). "Big data has become part of the problem." (Loukides, 2010).

Pegna (2015) stated, "To give you an idea of how much data needs to be processed, a medium-size network with 20,000 devices (laptops, smartphones, servers) will transmit more than 50 TB of data in a 24 hour period." Just looking at the data from a security point of view, that is over 5 GB of data that must be analyzed every second to detect cyberattack, potential threats, and malware attributed to malicious hackers!

Other examples of the very increasing size of "big data" include:

- 500 terabytes of new data per day are ingested in Facebook databases.
- At the CERN (European Organization for Nuclear Research), 1 petabyte of data is generated per second.
- The new Square Kilometer Array telescope will generate 1 exabyte of data per day.

III. WHAT IS DATA SCIENCE?

After reading, studying, and researching Data Science, I have come to understand the following statement: "Describing data science is like trying to describe a sunset - it should be easy, but somehow capturing the words is impossible." (Herman, 2013).

Pierson (2015) stated that "...data science represents process and resource optimization. Data science produces 'data insights' - insights you can use to understand and improve your business, your investments, your health...". Data Science is the ability to turn on the lights in a dark room.

Various articles define Data Science as the capacity to turn data into actions; this is a competitive advantage for organizations interested in winning in their selected field of endeavors. Most of the literature states that Data Science is a profession with a blended set of skills including; computer science, mathematics, statistics, visualization, human-centric analysis, and domain expertise (Markey, 2014). Someone who is a domain expert is more commonly referred as a Subject Matter Expert or SME and defined in Wikipedia as "A domain expert is a person with specialized knowledge or skills in a particular area of endeavor."

Data Science supports and encourages shifting between two separate domains simultaneously. One is hypothesis-based (deductive) and the second is pattern-based (inductive). In combining both deductive and inductive reasoning, an environment is created where models or reality no longer need to be static and empirically based.

This new combination allows for constant testing, updating, and improvement to the models being used to provide insight to the question being asked. Continuing this would allow a transformation of data into insights that help improve existing processes and decisions. Companies must develop data science teams to Maintain competitiveness in an increasingly data-rich environment.

IV. DATA SCIENCE KEY ACTIVITIES

Below is a brief review of the Obtain, Scrub, Explore, Model, and iNterpret (OSEMN) model (Mason, 2010) or "Key Activities" to be used for Data Science as listed in the "Field Guide to Data Science" (Herman, 2013). Herman states, "Data Science is a complex area. It is difficult, intellectually taxing work, which requires the sophisticated integration of talent, tools, and techniques." Having a model, (Mason, 2010) or the main activities checklist, (Herman, 2013) is a central theme to working with the complexities of Data Science.

OSEMN is a list of tasks a data scientist should be familiar with and comfortable using. Janssens (2015) points out that no data scientist will be an expert at all of them. The following is a discussion of OSEMN model, based on a 2010 post by Mason and Wiggins. Furthermore, this was the structure of a recent book entitled "Data Science at the Command

Line: Facing the Future with Time-Testing Tools" (Janssens, 2015). The following paragraphs intertwine the Key Activities checklist as discussed in the "Field Guide to Data Science" into the steps below from the OSEMN model. The Steps to OSEMN and Key Activities are:

Step	OSEMN	Key Activities
1	Obtaining data	Acquire
2	Scrubbing data	Prepare
3	Exploring data	Analyze
4	Modeling data	Act
5	Interpreting data	

Step 1. "Obtaining data" or "Acquire."

With today's large influence of data, a manual processing of data is not scalable, and we must learn to automate how we obtain the data needed to solve a given problem. Brownice (2014) states "... manual processing of data is like copying and pasting data with a mouse from one document to other. Mason and Wiggins (2010) "suggest that you adopt a range of tools and use the one most suitable for the job at hand." Examples included Linux command line tools, SQL in structured databases, web scraping and scripting using Python, Java, and JavaScript, and Linux shell scripts. Under the Key Activities listed (Herman, 2013), the first event is entitled "Acquire" and focuses on obtaining the data needed. Further, Herman states that all analysis starts with access to data and that "diversity is good and complexity is okay" and that the general guidance to acquiring data involves the following:

- Look inside first: don't filter your data.
- Remove the format constraints: think of unstructured and semi-structured data.
- Figure out what's missing: what data would make a difference.
- Embrace diversity: use both public and private data that is structured, unstructured, and semi-structured.

Step 2. "Scrubbing data" or "Prepare."

Data cleaning (scrubbing) or as Loukides (2010) called the process "data conditioning ... getting data into a state where it's usable" is necessary before analysis of data is possible. Data is frequently missing or incongruous. If data is missing, does the researcher ignore the missing points? If the data is incongruous, do you decide that something is wrong with poorly behaved data or that the unrelated data is telling its own story? (Loukides, 2010). The authors believe this is where data science shine, but showing how what appears to be "unrelated data" is in reality very related data.

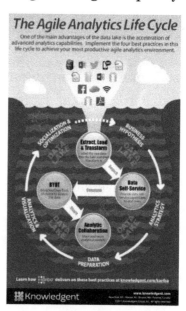

Figure 1. Data Lake Concept

Mason and Wiggins (2010) continue by stating that "Scrubbing data is the least sexy part of the analysis process, but often one that yields the greatest benefits." A simple analysis of clean data can be more productive than a complicated or convoluted algorithm of noisy and non-conforming data.

Under the Key Activities approach, once you have the data, you need to prepare it for analysis. Herman discussed a new approach to collecting, storing, and integrating data that he believes helps an organization maximize the utility of data. This method, being adopted by many companies, called "data lake," consolidates a complete repository of data into a single, broad and deep view. This method eliminates future expense known as Extract/Transform/Load (ETL). Three database functions are combined into one tool that pulls data out of one database and places it into another database. Figure 1 is an example of an Infographic illustrating the data lake concept and reduction of ETL time and cost.

Data scrubbing can be very basic and straightforward such as ensuring that the data is able to be read clearly, is stripped of extra characters and is parsed in a usable format. Mason and Wiggins (2010) provide an excellent example of "how messy the world is" with a simple geographic distribution of Twitter users by profile reporting. In this example, individuals living in New York City reported their location as "New York," "NY," "NYC," "New York City," "Manhattan, NY," "The Big Apple." This is the type of information that has to be scrubbed to reach a standard field for analysis or requires writing a program with every possible combination of New York City. Common tools that prove to be useful are sed, awk, grep for small tasks, and Peri and Python for larger data sets.

Step 3. Exploring data or "Analyze."
Exploring data is only looking at data. It has been called visualizing, clustering, or getting creative with performing dimensionality reduction. Normally these are exploratory with no hypothesis being made and no attempts at predictions. Exploring data is very useful in getting to know your data.

Under the Key Activities checklist, the "Analyze" activity requires the greatest effort of all activities in the Data Science endeavor. "The Data Scientist actually builds the analytics that creates value for data. Analytics in this context is an iterative application of specialized and scalable computational resources and tools to provide relevant insights from exponentially growing data." (Herman, 2010).

In exploring data from a security perspective, the Linux commands "more or less" or "awk" are useful. A single variable histogram that visually renders a single feature could be helpful, or a simple pair scatters plot to reveal characteristics of the data would work. Other tools that the security data scientist should bring into play during this phase are dimensionality reduction, Gaussian mixture modeling and possibly K-means.

Step 4. Modeling Data or "Act."

Both Brownice (2014) and Mason and Wiggins (2010) discussed why we build models to predict and to interpret. Both concluded that predictions could be assessed quantitatively and "more predictive is less bad," but with interpretation, it is simply a matter of which is less ugly. Whether in the natural sciences, engineering, or any data-rich environment, often the best model comes down to the most predictive model. The best way to frame questions of model selection is to remember why we build models in the first place: to predict and interpret.

Herman (2013) combined the last two steps of the OSEMN, "Modeling and iNterpreting" into a single step for the Key Activities, just called Act. The critical factor of the Key Activity checklist is our ability to make use of the analysis.

"The Field Guide to Data Science" provides some guiding principles to help frame the output for maximum impact for the decision maker. They are as follows:

- The finding must make sense with relatively little up-front preparation.
- The result must make the most meaningful patterns, trends, and exceptions easy to see and interpret.
- Every effort must be made to encode quantitative data accurately.
- The logic used to arrive at the finding must be clear.
- The findings must answer real business questions.

We are interested in the complexity of the model by comparing the value of loss functions and minimized generalization errors. Which one is the least wrong, because as Mason and Wiggins (2010) stated from work by Box, "all models are wrong, but some are useful." So, essentially we are choosing from a set of models that maximizes predictive power and is thus the least bad among our choices.

Step 5. Interpreting Data

Mason and Wiggins (2010) stated that "the purpose of computing is insight, not numbers." Interpreting data is a two-headed coin; on one side is the predictive power of modeling and its ability to generalize quantitative sense and to make accurate quantitative predictions of data in a new situation. The flip side is its ability to suggest to the modeler which would be the most interesting track to investigate next.

V. WHAT IS BIG DATA SECURITY OR SECURITY DATA SCIENCE?

In numerous writings about being a Data Scientist or forming a Big Data Team, there is the "subject matter expert." The following is a brief discussion on the security subject matter expert and Data Science.

In the last few years, there has been an explosion in the amount of data that's available to the network IT staff or computer security specialist. Whether we're talking about logs, internal or web servers, online transaction records, data from sensors, government data, etc. the problem isn't finding data, it's figuring out what to do with it (Loukides, 2015).

As previously cited, Data Science is a profession with a blended set of skills including computer science, mathematics, statistics, visualization, human-centric analysis, and domain expertise. Braxton (2012) added the subject domain of cyber security to this list to encompass Big Data Security.

An example of blending the skill set of Data Science with the skill set of Cyber Security is addressed in an article from Lewis University entitled "Data Science Meets Cyber Security" (Klump, 2014). In this the article, Klump discussed how the authors of the "2014 Verizon Data Breach Investigations Report" used a Data Science analysis technique called clustering, which categorized the incidents in terms of their similarities. Based on this method the authors (Verizon Data Breach Investigations Report) were able to group 92% of the incidents into only nine categories.

The Verizon team grouped attacks into clusters then described them in terms of predictive variables., Data Scientists, along with a security subject matter expert, were able to help organizations in the report understand which systems were vulnerable to attack. Then using advanced statistical tools, the Data Scientists were able to make an inference to who/what/when/how were responsible for the attacks. This analysis is based on "normal network behavior" for the company/industry as a whole.

When an organization looks at their data as a whole, they can plan their cyber security efforts based on verified data rather than on intuition, or worse, guesswork that relies on what has been done in the past.

The tools and techniques of the Security Data Scientist are no different than those used for

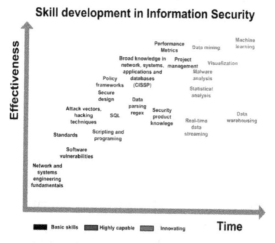

Figure 2. Skills Needed for Cyber Security Experts.

Data Science in any data domain. This group has a micro-focus on reducing risk and identifying fraud or malicious insiders using data science. Domain knowledge and experience are critical to successfully applying analytics to reduce risk and fraud losses. We believe developing Security Data Science is needed to bring together several security issues and fraud sub-domains under a combined practice, including advanced security metrics, visualization, and analytics (Curry, 2013).

Figure 2 (taken from the Association of Security Data Scientist dated early 2015) highlights some of the skills needed by today's cyber security experts. The Verizon 2014 Data Breach Investigations Report illustrates the intriguing opportunities for experts from Information Security and Data Science to collaborate these two critical fields.

The Association of Security Data Scientist (2015) website asks, "What is security data science?" It is the application of advanced analytics to activity and access data to uncover unknown risks. Generally, Data Science is the practice of deriving valuable insights from data and, in the world of security, these precious insights lead to reduced risk. Data Science is emerging to meet the challenges of processing vast data sets, i.e. "Big Data" and the explosion of new data generated from smart devices, the web, mobile and social media. Data Science has a long and rich history in security and fraud monitoring. The information security and fraud prevention industry has been evolving the field of Security Data Science to tackle the challenges of managing and gaining insights from massive streams of log data, discover insider threats and prevent fraud. Security Data Science is "data driven" meaning that new knowledge, value, and business goals come directly from the manipulation and interpretation of data.

I reiterate the Association of Security Data Scientists (2015) question "Why Security Data Science?" This is a subject matter expert that "is focused on advancing information security through practical applications of exploratory data analysis, statistics, machine learning and data visualization. Although the tools and techniques are no different than those used for data science in any data domain, this group has a micro-focus on reducing risk, identifying fraud or malicious insiders with data science methodologies. We believe domain knowledge and experience is critical to successfully applying analytics to reduce risk and fraud losses. The authors, think developing security data science is needed to bring together different security aspects and fraud sub-domains under a combined practice including Security Information and Event Management (SIEM) development, advanced security metrics, visualization, and analytics."

When Big Data drives security, the result is a unified, self-evolving approach and a holistic awareness that discrete, stitched-together solutions can't begin to achieve Curry (2013).

Now we understand that Security Data Scientists are just Data Scientists with a subject matter expertise in Cyber Security and that the tools and skill set are the same as any practitioner of Data Science, only focused in a particular field.

VI. DATA SCIENCE TOOLS

Many Data Science tools are either Open Source Tools for programming and statistical analysis in Data Science or Visualization Tools. A great place to review tools for big data is Harvey's 2012 article in the magazine Datamation entitled "50 Top Open Source Tools for Big Data."

VI. A. Open Source Programming and Statistical Analysis Tools

Security Data Scientists and data engineers use a variety of instruments. Most use Java, Python, R, and bash scripting to collect and analyze security data. The following is a short list of tools. However, new tools – frameworks, techniques, etc. – are being offered every day as Data Science continues to grow and develop:

- **Java** is ideal for larger data science tasks, per Hadoop and R (Markey, 2014). For machine learning, Markey suggests Mahout as the framework to develop the classification models and automation of the training and testing of these traditional models.

- **Python** is helpful for less intensive data science tasks but especially useful for working in a dynamic, changing environment. Python packages like psycopg provide a straight-forward interface with data sources (Markey, 2014). Another Application Program Interface (API) for security data science that should be investigated is VirusTotal. The VirusTotal website provides free checking of files for viruses. It uses up to 54 different antivirus products and scan engines to check for viruses that the user's own antivirus solution may have missed or to verify against any false positives.

- **R Project,** also known as **R Programming**, has become, like Hadoop, a backbone of Data Science investigations. Numerous authors have stated that R's strength lies in its variety of mathematical and statistical packages (Markey, 2014; Pierson, 2015). I would also agree with both of them that **R** is an excellent addition to any security data scientist toolbox. It has many of the most useful statistical tools in an easy to use programming language. **R** provides quick and easy methods for calculating the correlation between features to help down-select the most pertinent information for a model.

- **Hadoop** is another backbone of Data Science that was developed by the Apache Software Foundation. It is an open-source software framework written in Java for distributed storage and processing of massive data sets on computer clusters. Hadoop is currently the go-to program for handling massive volumes and varieties of data because it was designed to make large-scale computing more affordable and flexible. Pierson (2105) states that Hadoop is a great solution to handle, process, and group mass streams of structured, semi-structured, and unstructured data. Hadoop is not used for real-time streaming data solutions but still should be included in everyone's toolbox for Data Science.

- **MapReduce** is a programming paradigm that was designed to allow parallel distributed processing of large sets of data, converting them to sets of tuples, and then combining and reducing those tuples into smaller sets of tuples. Pierson, (2015) summed MapReduce up nicely by stating "... you can quickly and efficiently boil down and begin to make sense of a massive volume, velocity, and variety of data by using map and reduce tasks to tag your data by (key, value) pairs, and then reduce those pairs into smaller sets of data through aggregation operations - operations that combine multiple values from a dataset into a single value..." MapReduce can be used as part of a Hadoop solution.

- **NoSQL** was developed because the traditional Relational Database Management

Systems (RDBMS) are not designed or equipped to handle big data demands. The traditional relational databases were designed to handle only relational datasets that are constructed of data that can be stored in clearly defined rows and columns. The advantage of this is the capability of being able to query the database using Structured Query Language (SQL). An RDBM database is an example of a structured data set. In data science, we need to work with structured data, as well as unstructured and semi-structured data. Finally, RDBM systems just do not have the processing and handling capabilities that are needed for meeting big data "volume" and "velocity" requirements.

- When selecting a NoSQL database like MongoDB, remember that the purpose of these databases is to step out past the traditional relational database architecture and offer a more scalable, efficient solution. In addition, NoSQL offers four categories; graph databases, document databases, key-values stores, and column family stores to the mix of data interpretation.

- **Linux** command-lines provide built-in tools, like "Curl," "wget," "sed" and "grep," all handy for data science tasks. These commands are very helpful "in the collection of data, the analysis of features, and summarizing of content" (Markey, 2014). Other command-line tools are extremely useful for basic data science tasks that can be explored at a later date.

VI. B. Open Source Visualization Tools

Visualization allows the naked eye to detect

"A picture is worth a thousand packets." (McRee, 2008)

patterns and get insight about a network which could be missed by a purely statistical or mathematical approach. Visualizing data is the fun, artistic part of working with data, whether you are trying to show the data as a word cloud, treemap, histogram, scatter plot, raster surface map or dozens of different ways. You must first start by recognizing your audience. The

"If you focus only on the science aspect of Data Science you will never become a data artist." (Herman, 2013)

purpose of data visualization is to convey meaning and significance of the data, to provide insight into what the data means and how this data affects your company, project, or network.

To understand what the numbers mean, the stories they are actually telling, you need to generate a graph. Edward Tufte's <u>Visual Display of Quantitative Information</u> is the standard for data visualization and a

foundation text for anyone practicing Data Science. As Loukides (2010) states "Visualization is key to data conditioning and visualization is also frequently the first step in the analysis."

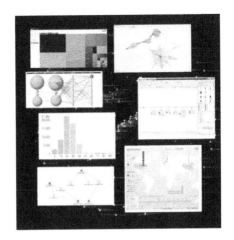

There are hundreds of open source visualization tools and applications available. Below is a small sampling.

- **InetVis** is a 3-D scatterplot tool that is in the category of network traffic visualization. This tool represents either live network traffic or recorded packet captures. Some limitations of InetVis are that the axis assignments are fixed, that you can only visualize source address, destination address, and destination port (Marty, 2010). InetVis may be downloaded at http://www.cs.ru.ac.za/research/g02v2468/inetvis.ht ml.

- **AfterGlow** is a tool which facilitates the process of generating graphs. It is the most downloaded security visualization tool. The tool is a collection of scripts that facilitate the process of creating link graphs. Written 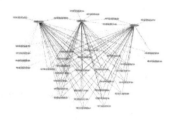 in Perl, it needs to be invoked using the command line. Afterglow may be downloaded at http://afterglow.sourceforge.net.

- **Rumint** takes captured traffic live from the network interface and visualizes it in various ways; some would say unconventional ways. It is used to analyze network traffic and to display the network behavior over time. Rumint may be downloaded at http://www.rumint.org/.

- **Treemap** is a space-constrained visualization of hierarchical structures. It is very effective in showing attributes of leaf nodes using 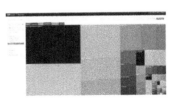 size and color coding. Treemap enables users to compare nodes and sub-trees, even at varying depth in the tree, and help users spot patterns and exceptions. Treemap may be downloaded at http://www.cs.umd.edu/hcil/treemap.

- **DAVIX** (Data Analysis and Visualization Linux) is a LiveCD for security visualization. 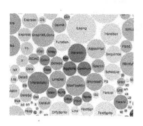"The idea behind DAVIX is to provide an integrated out-of-the-box environment for data and visualization analysis." McRee (2008) It comes pre-assembled with a set of 25 visualization tools and other essential tools for manipulating log files. The latest update to DAVIX is located at http://www.secviz.org/node/89. In addition to the original tools, the 2014 update to DAVIX included new or updated tools. For visualization flow tag, this includes Gephi, Google Earth, ELK Stack, PicViz, and AfterGlow. Other tools in the latest DAVIX update include DNS-browse, iPyhon, netsed, MSN-console, PRADS, R-studio, rsyslog, tcpstat, and teletraffic trapper. This is a logical starting point for anyone wanting to visualize data.

- **D3** is a JavaScript library for data-driven documents for producing dynamic, interactive data visualizations in web browsers. D3 makes use of the widely implemented SVG, HTML5, and CSS standard. D3 allows great control over the final visual results unlike many other libraries (Pierson, 2015).

For more examples of visualization tools see Chickowski (2013).

VII. APPLYING DATA SCIENCE TO CYBER SECURITY

In the past, cybersecurity was based on signatures of the malware. Now, with the structural transition from signature patterns to behavior abnormality for malware, identification is the biggest enabler of applying Data Science to cyber security. Intrusion Prevention System (IPS) and Next-Generation Firewall (NGFW) perimeter security solutions inspect network traffic for matches with a signature that has been created in response to analysis of specific malware samples. In our laboratory, we were able to make minor changes to malware that reduced the effectiveness or evaded the IPS and NGFW. In another experiment, we used 10-year-old viruses that easily evaded the IPS and NGFW current signatures, because old viruses are no longer part of the signatures library. When we used the behavior method, machines infected with malware were identified through the observations of their abnormal behavior. Identifying abnormal behavior requires primarily the capability of first determining what's normal and using data science's analytical methods to identify anomalies. The above illustrates that applying the data science approach is useful on small-scale investigations of cyber security.

One of the first steps of moving into using the Data Science approach is that an organization must gain full visibility into the security conditions of all digital assets that are handling valuable information (Curry, 2013). Furthermore, "when big data drives security, the results are significantly enhanced visibility into IT  environments and the ability to distinguish suspicious from regular activities to inspire trust in our IT system."

Another example of the behavior approach to using Data Science is using Wireshark to capture network packets, then using Hadoop and/or R to help process and then graphically identify where packets are originating using the various mapping open source software. That information is then visualized so the packet traffic can be understood.

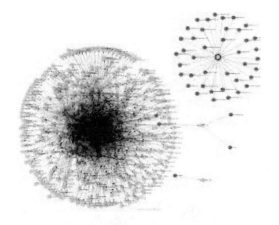

"Most users have minimal understanding of security threats." (Tamassia 2009). Tamassia continues with ... "the field of security visualization has emerged to provide novel ways to security-related information so that it is easier to understand."

Intrusion Detection visualization of a network helps to identify machines that have tried to gain unauthorized access to other machines. This approach consists of packet collecting, clustering, and event generation. By overlaying packets collected and clustered over time, an intrusion methodology can be learned using regression testing in R.

Access Control assists security data scientists in understanding complex policies that access control mechanisms enforce. This approach is used to answer questions about what individual or group has access to files and when. The application of RubaViz was reviewed by Tamassia and his team at Brown University. RubaViz, a visualization software that constructs a diagram for the administrator with subjects (people or processes), resources and groups.

Attack Graphs are used to represent attack paths that an adversary can exploit to compromise a system. Efficient visualization of attack graphs helps computer security analysts identify and fix vulnerabilities. Using clustering techniques standard in data science, the researchers at Brown University used a network and a database of known vulnerabilities that applied to certain parts of the network. Each edge in the graph is an exploit of a particular vulnerability that allows the attacker to move from one machine to another.

These examples have just touched the surface of applying Data Science and Visualization to security. Much, much more could be written.

We will continue our research into the world of security Data Science.

VIII. Conclusion

Our world has never been as interconnected as it is today. We freely share our day-to-day lives on social media. We conduct personal and corporate business dealings while bits and parts of the details are stored in databases and shared in ways we can't imagine. All of these tidbits are crunched together to create a myriad of data - Big Data.

As scary as all this sounds, data science doesn't have to be the boogie man. Industry professionals must be aware of the inherent risks of gathering data and protect it from those who would do harm. The information gleaned can make our lives easier by tracking health trends, recognizing financial changes, stopping cyber theft, and presenting complex data in easily interpreted visuals. Books and articles over the last few years indicate that security solutions are now adopting data science techniques and methodologies. Herman (2013) posits that "Data science capabilities are creating data analytics that is improving every aspect of our lives, from life-saving disease treatments to national security, to economic stability, and even the convenience of selecting a restaurant."

In contrast, the use of advanced analytical techniques, big data, and all the traditional components that have become representative of data science have not been at the center of cyber security solutions focused on identification and prevention of cyber-attacks (Pegna, 2015). Curry (2013) predicts big data analytics will disrupt the status quo in most information security projects including Security Information and Event Management (SIEM), network monitoring, fraud detection, and risk.

In integrating data science into security, an organization should consider the following steps (Curry, 2013):
1. Set a holistic cyber security strategy

2. Establish a shared data architecture for security information
3. Migrate from point products to a unified security architecture
4. Look for open and scalable big data tools
5. Strengthen security specialists' data science skills
6. Leverage external threat intelligence

Technical experts in cyber security cannot depend on any one tool or process to do their part in these efforts. Applying data science techniques and methodologies against sophisticated adversaries is a process that needs to be explored, developed, and implemented to safeguard our networks. The amount of data being gathered is mind-boggling and ever-growing. There are many open source tools available to aid in creating viable data analysis while keeping the information safe. Undoubtedly, that list will continue to grow.

Hopefully, the information shared here will help you become the catalyst for your organization, leading the inclusion of data science to protect, predict, and prevent cyber-attacks on your network.

Predictive Cyber Threat Analysis using Data Science

10 REFERENCES

Books

Marty, Raffael (2009). Applied Security Visualization. Upper Saddle River, NJ: Pearson Education, Inc.

Pierson, Lillian (2015). Data Science for Dummies. Hoboken, NJ: John Wiley & Sons, Inc.

Janssens, Jeroen (2015). Data Science at the Command Line. Sebastopol, CA: O'Reilly Media, Inc.

Articles (not all articles listed are cited in the paper, but provide useful background knowledge)

2014 Data Breach Investigations Report (2014). Verizon: Retrieved from http://www.verizonenterprise.com/DBIR/2014/reports/rp_dbir-2014-executive-summary_en_xg.pdf

Association of Security Data Science (ASDS) (unknown). Security Data Science. Retrieved from http://securitydatascience.org/

Braxton, Paul (January 20, 2015) Institute of Cyber Threat Management (IOCTM). Traditional Information Security approach must evolve to manage cyber threats. Cyber Threat Management Framework (CTMF). Retrieved from https://www.ioctm.org/Blog/3205303

Brownice, Jason (December 19, 2014). How to work through a problem lie a data scientist. Retrieved from /http://machinelearningmastery.com/how-to-work-through-a-problem-like-a-data-scientist/

Chickowski, Ericka (December 31, 2013). Slide Show: 8 Effective Data Visualization Methods For Security Teams Retrieved from http://www.darkreading.com/slide-show-8-effective-data-visualization-methods-for-security-teams/d/d-id/1141113?

Corthell, Clare (2014). The Open Source Data Science Masters. Retrieved from http://DataSciencemasters.org

Curry, Sam (January 2013). Big Data Fuels Intelligence-Driven Security. Retrieved from http://www.emc.com/collateral/industry-overview/big-data-fuels-intelligence-driven-security-io.pdf

Harvey, Cynthia (2012). Datamation. Retrieved from http://www.datamation.com/data-center/50-top-open-source-tools-for-big-data-1.html

Herman, Mark, Rivers, Stephanie, Mills, Steven, Sullivan, Josh, Guerra, Peter, Cosmas, Alex (2013) The Field Guide to Data Science. McLean, Virginia: Booz, Allen, Hamilton

Loukides, Mike (2015) What is Data Science? An O'Reilly Radar Report: O'Reilly Media, Inc. Retrieved from http://radar.oreilly.com/

Kar, Saroj (February 12, 2014). Gartner Report: Big Data will Revolutionize Cyber Security in the next Two Years. Retrieved from http://cloudtimes.org/2014/02/12/gartner-report-big-data-will-revolutionize-the-cybersecurity-in-next-two-year/

Klump, Ray (October 11,2014). Data Science Meets Cyber Security. Retrieved from Lewis

University
http://www.lewisu.edu/experts/wordpress/index.php/d
ata-science-meets-cyber-security/

Knowledge Perspectives May 19, 2015.
Knowledgent's Data Lake White Paper Cited in
Information Management's Data Lakes Guide.
Retrieved from
http://blog.knowledgent.com/knowledgents-data-lake-
white-paper-cited-in-information-managements-data-
lakes-guide/

Janssens, Jeroen (2015). Data Science Toolbox.
Retrieved from http://datasciencetoolbox.org

Markey, Jeff (June 23, 2014). What Does a
Security Data Scientist do? Retrieved from
ThreatTrack Security.
http://www.threattracksecurity.com/blogs/cso/security-
data-scientist/

Mason, Hilary and Chris Wiggins (September
25, 2010). The Taxonomy of Data Science.
Retrieved from Dataists
http://www.dataists.com/2010/09/a-taxonomy-of-data-
science/

McRee, Russ (June 2008). Security
Visualization: What you don't see can hurt you.
ISSA Journal: Retrieved from http://www.issa.org

Novert, Jordan (December 13, 2013) DataTau launches as a Hacker News for data scientists. VB News. Retrieved from http://venturebeat.com/2013/12/13/datatau-launches-as-a-hacker-news-for-data-scientists/

O'Brien, Ted (June 16,2014). 50+ Open Source Tools for Big Data. Data Science Report - Today! Retrieved from http://datasciencereport.com/2014/06/16/50-open-source-tools-for-big-data-see-anything-missing/#.VZBGJOGc1f8

Pegna, David (March 12, 2015). Big Data sends cybersecurity back to the future. Computerworld. Retrieved from http://www.computerworld.com/article/2893656/the-future-of-cybersecurity-big-data-and-data-science.html

Pegna, David (February 20, 2015). Creating Cybersecurity that thinks. Computerworld. Retrieved from http://www.computerworld.com/article/2881551/creating-cyber-security-that-thinks.html

Security Data Science (2015) Retrieved from Association of Security Data Scientist http://www.securitydatascience.org/

Sivaprasad, Rohit (2015). Datatau: Hacker News for Data Science Retrieved from http://www.datatau.com

Tamassia, Roberto, Bernardo Palazzi, Charalampos Papamanthou (2009) Graph Drawing for Security Visualization. Brown University: Retrieved from http://citeseerx.ist.psu.edu/viewdoc/download?rep=rep1&type=pdf&doi=10.1.1.212.5669

Woodie, Alex (April 9, 2015). Why Cybersecurity Needs Big Data Tech, Especially Hadoop Retrieved from Datanami http://www.datanami.com/2015/04/09/why-cybersecurity-needs-big-data-tech-especially-hadoop/

ABOUT THE AUTHORS

Mr. Hale is a Computer Scientist with a substantial depth and breadth of experiences, totaling 32 years, in Software Engineering, System Administration, Security Engineering, Cyber Warfare, Information Assurance, Cognitive System Engineering, Test and Evaluation (T&E), Independent Verification and Validation (IV&V), Command, Control, Communications, Computers, Intelligence, Surveillance, and Reconnaissance (C4ISR), and Situational Awareness.

Currently, Mr. Hale is both a System Administrator (SysAdm) and Information System Security Officer (ISSO) who manages several (5) classified laboratories for various programs, including U.S. Navy and Missile Defense Agency (MDA).

As the Cyber Technical Lead, Mr. Hale is involved in the implementation of both Defense Federal Acquisition Regulation Supplement (DFARS) and Risk Management Framework (RMF). He researches trends in cognitive neuroscience, cyber security, and cyber warfare.

Mr. Hale predominantly utilizing an interdisciplinary approach that brings the human side to technology by combining Cognitive and Behavioral Science, with Computer and Security Engineering.

Additionally, Mr. Hale has 22 years of teaching experience, including the past 15 years as an Adjunct Professor of Computer Science where he teaches courses in System Security Management, Digital Forensics, Cyber Ethics, and Javascript and others. He is the author of five books, numerous white papers and presentations for various conferences and professional gathering.

You may contact Mr. Hale at ProfessorHale@gmail.com or AbbyNormalResearch@gmail.com

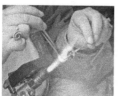

Ms. Terry Hale has been fascinated with the decision-making process since she began dealing with customers in her family's business when she was a young teen. Throughout her adult life, she has studied social engineering while working in a career that includes sales, teaching, corporate training, and NASA and Department of Defense technical support.

Currently, Terry is a full-time glass artist and jewelry designer. Her designs can be found in fine art galleries and shows throughout the southeast US. In addition to teaching in her studio, Terry regularly teaches at John C. Campbell Folk School in Brasstown NC, Appalachian Center for Craft (Tennessee Tech) in Smithville TN, and at Essence of Mulranny, County Mayo, Ireland. She depends on her study of cognitive biases while teaching and decision making while selling her artwork.

You contact Terry at terry@halefireglass.com or AbbyNormalResearch@gmail.com

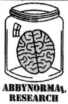

ABBYNORMAL
RESEARCH

Other books by SA and Terry Hale

Common Cognitive Biases: Examples and Challenges
ISBN: 1533298122

Hacker Profiling: An Overview of Approaches
ASIN: B071DZC8K7

Predictive Cyber Threat Analysis using Data Science
ISBN: 1546727841

Winning Management Buy-in to Security
ISBN: 1541271807
Final Editing estimated publishing date: Mid June 2017

Social Engineering: A Practitioner Guide
In Process Estimated publishing date November 2017